FISH OUT OF WATER

THE GUIDE TO ACHIEVING BREAKTHROUGH AND PERMANENTLY TRANSFORMING INTO THE NEW YOU

CALVIN WAYMAN

DEDICATION

To my **PARENTS** for teaching me to work hard and stand up for what I believe in...

To **BEKAH** for always supporting me...

To **ARCHIE** for reminding me that happiness lives in the present moment...

To the **LITTLE BOY INSIDE ME**, always dreaming, always believing...

To the entrepreneur in **YOU**.

CONTENTS

FOREWORD

By Calvin's Coach and Mentor, Nick Unsworth

Hey hey! If you're reading this right now it tells me that you're on a mission—on a mission to take your life and career to a whole new level and for that...I commend you.

As an entrepreneur of seventeen years, I know exactly what it's like to be a *fish out of water*. I spent my twenties flipping and flopping gasping for air (and money) as I clung to the "hope" that I would eventually make it.

Thank God I did. After eleven business failures, I realized that I had been doing it all wrong. I was pursuing money without pursuing "purpose."

The "ah-ha" moment came when I was $50,000 in debt and struggling to survive. I took a risk and borrowed money to hire my first mentor. At that point, my boats were burned…shoot they were absolutely smoldering!

With debt and financial pressure collapsing all around me, I made a decision that I was going to make it. That decision was followed by a goal I tattooed on my chest that I would sell a business within two years—even though I had absolutely no idea what the new business would be.

For the first time in my career, I got out of my own way and let a mentor guide me. Surrendering control and having faith that it would all work out was the rocket fuel that got me up in the air.

Since then, I did successfully sell the business within two years in 2012 (woo-hoo!) and I started LifeonFire.com to help others realize their true potential and dreams.

When I look back, it is clear as day that there are three very distinct strategies that changed everything for me and they will change everything for you as well.

1. Consistent Imperfect Action

As a Peak Performance Coach, I often tell my clients "done beats perfect" because if you wait until your ideas are perfect the opportunity will pass you by and you'll end up floundering and gasping for air.

2. Hire a Coach & Surround Yourself with Top Performers

When I was dead broke and invested $5,000 to hire a coach and join a mastermind, everything changed. I went from trying to do it all on my own to gaining strength from others. I learned from people that had actually done it before me. Most importantly, I surrounded myself with people who were smarter than me. The tide raises all boats!

3. Personal Development

Whether you're an entrepreneur or someone who is on a mission in your career…your biggest enemy in life will inevitably be you. If you don't master what's between your ears the road to success will be very long and bumpy. Life is way too short to wait until some end destination to be happy and successful. Make the decision today to commit to your personal growth and development. Everything stems from that.

What I love about these three principles is that when someone actually implements them it creates radical growth and success. I know this from personal experience and it was so profound that I ended up becoming a business coach so that I could help others achieve their wildest dreams as well.

On my journey coaching over 2,500 people up to this point in my life, I am so grateful that Calvin Wayman is one of them. There has been nothing more fulfilling than to see Calvin go from a *fish out of water* gasping for air to growing into a powerful, successful leader with a heart and mind of solid gold. Calvin is living proof that you can achieve literally anything that you put your mind to.

The best part is that the ripple effect continues…

I went from broke and on the edge of financial collapse to making millions. Calvin went from broke and floundering, to courageously pursuing his dreams while helping many, many people along the way. Now, Calvin is in the fortunate position to share these very important gifts with you.

The one thing I ask is this…do not stop the ripple effect. Take what Calvin is teaching and you will radically change your life and career. Then go out and share these strategies with the world.

Be bold. Be courageous. Be Unstoppable!

Nick Unsworth
Life On Fire

To watch a full interview with my mentor, Nick Unsworth, and me go to TheFishOutOfWaterBook.com/LOF

INTRODUCTION

My first *fish out of water* experience.

At the age of twenty-three, in 2011, I read my first business and personal development book—Robert Kiyosaki's *Rich Dad, Poor Dad*. It blew my mind! I loved it! Something that stuck out to me was the emphasis on selling, and the need to develop the skill to sell. Robert Kiyosaki said it doesn't matter what you do in life or business, if you're going to be successful, you need to know how to sell.

As an aspiring entrepreneur, I loved what I had read. I always wanted to be an entrepreneur. I wanted freedom. I wanted to have my own business some day. I wanted to be in charge of my own life. So when I read *Rich Dad, Poor Dad,* I took the lessons seriously. I decided to go into sales. After a short while, I started working at a startup call-center called PlusOne, based out of Salt Lake City, UT to learn how to sell.

I was so excited! Because I had the "entrepreneur fire," I thought I would be a natural at sales. I sat anxiously through the sales training on the edge of my seat. I was so fascinated by what I was learning. It sounded like magic. I could hardly wait to get on the phones and start selling! Sales would be a perfect fit for me. As a new entrepreneur, I would do great right out of the gate, right?

Boy, was I mistaken. Reality hit me and I fell flat on my face! In my first couple of months, I managed to break the company record for the *worst* performance a sales agent ever had! Saying I was *horrible* at sales would be a massive understatement. I could hardly believe it. I was genuinely confused. My poor performance certainly wasn't for a lack of trying. I was working my face off. Sales was just completely new territory for me. Coming from a construction background, I was totally out of my element. At times I felt like I could barely breathe. I felt like I wasn't going to make it. I felt like a *fish out of water*.

I started to realize just how weird and unnatural this really was: talking to people on the phone, explaining products I didn't even know existed a few weeks prior, and actually trying to convince people to give me, a complete stranger, their credit card number? It was all so intimidating. Like a *fish out of water* I could barely breathe, let alone speak clearly and persuasively over the phone!

Then one day, for obvious reasons, the founder of the company, Marion Timpson, summoned me into his office. I went in with my tail tucked between my legs. Maybe this was it. I was about to get fired.

"These numbers are quite impressive!" he began. Knowing how badly I was actually performing, I looked on rather surprised and confused. "This is the lowest performance I've ever seen," he continued. "I don't know how you managed to achieve this. In a way, I'm quite impressed. I can't explain how you did it. I've never seen anything like it. I mean, if you just *read the script* you'll convert higher than this. I just don't know how you have achieved such great failure."

I was stumped. I was defeated. I had been costing the company money every single time I answered a phone call. I didn't know how to reply. It wasn't that I was a good employee gone bad. I hadn't even gotten started yet. I was a plane that hadn't even left the runway. "Obviously, this can't continue," Marion explained. "Either you have to fix this fast, or we just have to call it what it is."

"Call it what it is," was code for getting let go—I would be fired. Something had to change, and something had to change now! But what? Sitting in silence for a few seconds, I thought about why I was there in the first place. I remembered what Robert Kiyosaki said in *Rich Dad, Poor Dad*, that to be successful in life you need to know how to sell. My dreams and wishes of being an entrepreneur flashed in my mind. I wanted freedom. I wanted to know how to sell. I needed to know how to sell. That's why I was there. I wanted it badly!

"You said you could teach me to be the best!" I suddenly shot at Marion. He just stared at me. It surprised me that he *wasn't* surprised. Meekly, I continued, "You know, in your training? You said you could teach me to become a pro like you."

The corner of Marion's mouth created a little smirk. "I can," he said confidently. "The only question is, are you willing to learn what it takes to dominate at sales?"

"Yes, of course!" I replied eagerly. "That's why I'm here!"

"Okay then," Marion said calmly. "I'll make you a deal. Obviously, something has to change and this can't continue. The thing I love about you, Calvin, is you're young. You're raw. You're moldable. I know I can teach you. So if you promise to do everything I tell you to do, then I'll keep you. I'll make you my little experiment. And if you don't, then we part ways. Deal?"

Marion was a shark at sales. A *shark* is a pro with unusual skill—someone who is at a completely different standard from everyone else. He had worked for a call-center for years. He studied sales like a science and broke all kinds of records for his insanely great performance. He ultimately quit his job and started his own call-center. I knew he could teach me. "Deal!" I said excitedly. I had been given the chance. With the help of Marion as my new mentor and coach, I knew I could be successful. I, too, could become a shark.

It's been several years now since that meeting. It put me on the path to discovering things about myself I never knew. I learned, for the first time, what it meant to be a *fish out of water*, and what it took to transform into a shark. **A *fish out of water* is someone whose comfort zone has been stretched in pursuit of leveling up in some aspect of his or her**

life. It's something that is never experienced by people who stay inside their "normal"— guppies as I call them. A guppy is someone who stays inside his or her fishbowl of mediocrity—where it's comfortable. It's when you aim higher and pursue your dream of leaving the fishbowl where you feel like a *fish out of water*. That's exactly what happened when I started working at that call-center. My comfort zone was completely stretched! I knew I wanted to become a sales expert. I wanted to become a shark. I went after the goal. But as soon as I started taking action on my dream, I left my normal and it felt awkward.

I used principles I share in this book to get through the *fish out of water* stage and level up my sales game in a huge way. The road was rocky. But, in less than six months, I achieved the top performance rank (a 10, on a scale of 0-10). In a company with around 250 agents, I would consistently perform in the top three and ultimately hit the number 1 spot. The best part was, by the end it felt totally normal—a *new* normal. Selling was no longer intimidating. It didn't feel weird at all. I had hit breakthrough.

Years later, I started to wonder how it happened. How did I create a new standard of success when I started out so poorly? It's been several years since my sales experience, and I've been fortunate to use the same principles for different areas of my life. When I struggled to get into shape, I used these principles to create a new standard for my health. When I was afraid and confused about stepping into an entrepreneur role, I used these principles to become an entrepreneur. When I didn't know how to start a business, I used these principles to become a business owner. The same principles work in any area of life you're aiming to level up to. Whether you're looking to transform your career, your finances, or your relationships, these principles are for you. If you're an employee, a manager, a CEO, a network marketer, or an entrepreneur, these principles are for you.

Goals aren't enough.

You might be thinking, "I've tried to set and hit goals before and nothing worked. How is this book going to be different?" When going after a new goal, have you ever noticed how you get to this point where it feels like you just hit a wall? Have you ever been frustrated because you didn't know what to do next, or you wondered why it feels so hard? You can't explain it, but you got excited enough to set a goal only to hit this period that felt confusing at best, and downright suffocating at worst. You're not alone. You became a *fish out of water*. There are many books out there on goal-setting, and how to build yourself the perfect life. We've been taught that to achieve higher levels of success we must become great at setting goals. But why is it that goals are so often set but almost never met? Why do people struggle to have the level of success they so desire? Goals are not the only answer.

There's a missing piece that isn't talked about. Something happens to every person that dares to aim higher. When you are bold enough to set a goal and go after it you will become a *fish out of water*. As a *fish out of water* you feel like you're floundering. You'll feel awkward. You'll feel like you can barely breathe. And the truth is, just as a real fish can't be out of water for long. neither can you! You must either revert back to what feels normal (being a guppy) or you must break through the *fish out of water* stage and create a completely new version of yourself. A guppy's life is very limited and can only handle calm environments. A shark, on the other hand, dominates the water it swims in. It can handle rougher waters, and has a lot more space to move. A shark is confident, knows where it's going, and demands anything it wants. That's what this book is designed to help you become.

The three principles.

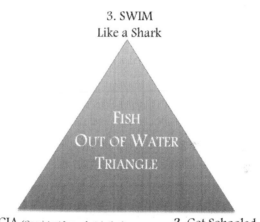

3. SWIM
Like a Shark

FISH
OUT OF WATER
TRIANGLE

1. CIA (Consistent Imperfect Action)   2. Get Schooled

By using these three principles you will create a new standard for yourself. You'll achieve breakthrough and permanently transform into a new you. These principles protect you from reverting back to a fishbowl of mediocrity and will take you from a *fish out of water* to a shark.

CIA—Consistent Imperfect Action.

Nothing happens without action. Most importantly, the key to beginning your transformation is through action. In the first section of this book, you'll discover myths about action and how making progress is way easier than you think.

Get Schooled.

In the second section, you'll learn what it means to "get schooled." A school in fish terms is a group of fish that stay together and swim in the same direction. You'll discover how getting around the right kinds of people will dramatically accelerate your transformation.

SWIM like a shark.

SWIM stands for Success, Words, Improve, and Measure. In the final section, you'll learn how sharks—successful people— use these four critical areas so you too can continually stay on top of your game.

You picked up this book for a reason. I designed *Fish Out of Water* to be a quick read that could be consumed on a one-way plane trip. Whether you are looking to get into better shape, improve your sales, transform your finances, become an entrepreneur, become a top network marketer, or any other transformation, the principles in this book are for you. I hope that they are as life changing for you as they have been for me.

Let's dive in!

SECTION 1

C.I.A.
CONSISTENT
IMPERFECT
ACTION

ALL SUCCESSFUL PEOPLE HAVE BEEN
MEMBERS OF THE C.I.A. WHEN YOU'RE
A *FISH OUT OF WATER*, DOING
SOMETHING FOR THE FIRST TIME FEELS
WEIRD AND MAKES YOU WANT TO
REVERT BACK TO WHAT FEELS NORMAL.
THE PRINCIPLES IN THIS FIRST SECTION
WILL HELP YOU BUILD MOMENTUM TO
BECOME THE SHARK YOU'RE MEANT TO
BE.

CHAPTER 1

NIKE HAD IT RIGHT

Even if you're on the right track, you'll still get run over if you don't keep moving.

In Spring 2015, I again became a *fish out of water*. I did something I wanted to do for years and finally built up enough courage to pull the trigger. I quit my day job to pursue my dream of working for myself. I was going after my calling of being an entrepreneur—of becoming a shark.

This leap was very new territory for me. Fear had kept me stuck in an employee role for a long time. Since I held myself back for so long, I could hardly believe I was now actually doing it! Why now? What changed in Spring 2015 to cause me to jump? What happened that created the courage to get me moving? Nothing. That's right. Nothing. Did I magically know exactly what to do? Nope. Did someone wave a magic wand over me and make me feel courageous? I wish. Instead, I just did it. I just starting taking small, consistent imperfect action.

Grant Cardone, a mentor of mine, wrote a book called *The 10X Rule*. I read this book when I quit my job. What I learned from *10X* is that one of the main problems that keeps people from having the success they want in life is they don't take enough *action*. They don't take action because they're worried, afraid, or they don't think they know the right steps to take. This was certainly true for me. Ironically, though, by *not* taking action, people stay stuck in the problems they're in. Progress requires *movement*. Progress requires *action*. Massive action. Consistent action. So that's what I started to do. I took Grant Cardone's advice and got in the game.

The best thing you can do when you are a *fish out of water* is to keep taking action—it is the remedy to overcome the temptation of reverting back to what feels normal and comfortable. Let me squash the myth that causes people to stay in the fishbowl of mediocrity and is responsible for murdering millions of dreams. We've been taught that the actions you take must be *just right*. You have to be careful. If you take the wrong actions, it could cost you everything.

That's a load of bull. What will cost you everything is *not* taking action. Realizing this is what caused me to quit my job. I projected myself ten years in the future and I asked my older self, "What should I do? What would happen if I *didn't* take action?" The idea of waking up ten years later and being in the same place was almost like suicide to me. Or worse, the idea that really got to me was thought of the entrepreneur fire inside of me *dying*. The fear of that happening swallowed the smaller fear of "just doing it." My older self also told me that if there was ever a time to go after my dream, it was now. We get more responsibility as we get older, not less. So if you're ever going to do it, do it now.

I recently attended an event where I got to listen to millionaire investor Robert Herjavec of *Shark Tank* speak. On this point, he said, "The biggest thing that kills a new business is they get stuck and then don't take enough action. You've got to get off the couch and stay off the couch. And it doesn't have to be perfect. *Action* is always better than *inaction*. Get moving. Go. Going is good."

Just "Jump."

Steve Harvey has a popular video on YouTube entitled "Jump." In the video, Mr. Harvey shares wisdom with his studio audience. He explains that every successful person in this world has "jumped." He goes on to explain that it doesn't matter where you come from, if you want to be successful, you're going to have to jump. As a viewer, you begin to get curious what he means by jumping. Jumping is taking a "leap of faith." Jumping is taking the next step. Jumping is not knowing if you're going to be safe but you take action anyway.

The only way to find your true gift, explains Steve Harvey, is by jumping. You have to jump off the cliff of life and that's when your parachute opens. Your parachute is your gift. But the only way for you to find out what your gift is, you've got to jump.

When I quit my day job in Spring 2015, it was a scary time for me to say the least! But the decision to jump—to quit my employee job and pursue my dream of working for myself—is what put me on the path I'm on today. It's also the reason you're even reading this book. Just jump.

I bring up this story with Steve Harvey because often times as a *fish out of water*, it's going to feel like you're in the dark. You know you need to take action, but you don't know *what* action. As Steve Harvey says, though, you just have to jump, even if it *is* in the dark. Know that whatever your goal or dream is, you can't sit around waiting for the right time to act on it. There is no right time. Just thinking about it positively will not bring it into your life. You have to take that action. You have to jump. That's when the magic happens. That's how you find your gift.

Does that mean it will suddenly be easy? Near the end of the video, Steve Harvey gives a caution—"let me be real with you," he says, "when you jump, your parachute (your gift) will not open right away. I wish I could tell you it did, but it doesn't. At first, you're going to hit them rocks. You're going to get some skin tore off on them cliffs, and you're going to be bleeding pretty bad." In other words, you're going to be a *fish out of water*. It's not going to feel normal at first. You're going to go through struggle and suffering. This is the

part that not very many people talk about. In
the beginning you may feel like you can
barely breathe. It's normal.

The great news is, "eventually," Steve
Harvey assures, "eventually the parachute
HAS to open and it will!" The key is, you
have to take action even before you're ready.
That's how you really start to find your gift.
You WILL find your gift. But if you don't
jump first, you'll never know what your gift
is. You'll only find it by jumping.

As mentioned earlier, I went many years
not utilizing my gifts. I stayed in an employee
job. I let fear hold me on the cliff of life. But
when I finally "jumped" and got in the game,
that made things start to click and form
together. So, even before you're ready, get in
the game. Just jump.

Plans are worthless if you aren't in the game.

At this point you might be thinking,
"well, if I'm going to really go after my goals
and dreams, I need to come up with a solid
game plan, then I'll get moving." That's
sounds like a good idea. But honestly, that's
one of the quickest ways to cause you to

revert back to being a guppy—someone comfortable in their mediocrity. You aren't meant to know what to do before you take the action, you take the action and then you know what to do.

Most plans suck. But even when they don't suck, they actually end up doing the opposite of what they were intended to do in the first place. I know, because I was so much this way! As a guppy, I was a planner. I planned and I planned and I planned! Do you want to know the one thing that plans did for me? (Apart from feeling warm and cozy because they made me feel like I was doing the right thing.) Plans kept me frozen. They didn't create simplicity and confidence. They created overwhelm.

Planning was okay when I was thinking about the first couple of steps I should take. But as the steps got further from the present moment, what I should do became fuzzier and fuzzier. Until, eventually, I wasn't even sure I wanted to go down that path after all. It led to so much uncertainty!

Then I realized I was doing it wrong. Plans don't work unless you're in the game. In fact, since I barely used the word "game," let's use sports to clarify this. Imagine you're in a basketball game. The "plan" is to win. You might even have a great strategy to help you win. But as soon as you get on the court, that plan goes to hell. Why? Because of all the many unpredictable factors. Unpredictable factors tear plans to shreds!

There's a famous quote from Mike Tyson that perfectly explains this, "Everyone has a plan until they get punched in the face." That's so real! Plans assume every factor is fixed and holding still. That sounds cool. But that's simply not how life is. To create great results, you get in the game, rely on your basic fundamentals, and take the next best action based on the context in front of you.

By the way, you learn based on context. Have you ever had someone try to explain the rules of a board game to you? Did you notice how it sounded totally confusing? You didn't really "get it" until you started playing the game. Then it became super easy! It's because, in the game, you now had context. That's how life is.

Done is better than perfect.

There's an old idea that says, "If something is worth doing, it's worth doing well." When you're a *fish out of water*, this is one of the most deadly ideas that can keep you stuck. It's a lie that kills progress. If something is worth doing, it's worth doing *poorly*.

Think about every skill you've developed since you were a child—from talking, to riding a bicycle, to typing, learning to drive, even reading, etc! Did you do it perfectly the first time? If you're a mere mortal like the rest of us the answer is an emphatic "no!" When you are doing something for the first time, you're going to mess up. It's not going to go right. It's going to be done poorly—and guess what, that's okay.

We knew this as children. We knew it was okay to play, experiment, and have fun. But somewhere along the way we became conditioned that the only acceptable result was perfection. In school, if we messed up we got bad grades. We learned that mistakes were bad. That caused us to be overly careful. Inevitably, and ironically, it didn't cause us to create perfect results; it just made us freeze. And no action equals no progress.

As dreamers, we, of course, believe that things can be much better than they are. We want things to be perfect. As such, we become our own worst critic. We want to be perfect. But wanting everything to be perfect is what all too often makes our idea sit on the shelf. Progress stops. It's important to realize this truth: ***done is better than perfect.***

So what should you do? Instead of aiming to be perfect, you need to FOC more. Yes, I said you need to FOC more. FOC equals "focus on completion." When you focus on *completion* instead of *perfection*, you will keep progressing instead of freezing.

Will Rogers said, "Even if you're on the right track, you'll still get run over if you just sit there." Knowing you're on the right path doesn't do you any good if you don't move. Don't just sit there. Get moving. Focus on completion. If something's worth doing, it's worth doing poorly. Imagine yourself in ten years. What would happen if you *didn't* take action?

New problems are a good thing.

One big reason we don't take action is we fear new problems that could arise. I already mentioned one of Grant Cardone's books and I've got another one for you. In *Sell or Be Sold*, Grant Cardone explains that new problems are actually a good thing, and they are. Most people avoid new problems like the plague and that's why they aren't where they want to be. Do you think sharks don't have problems? Of course, they do! The difference is this: sharks have much higher-level issues than guppies do. You *want* new problems. If you're dealing with the same old problems day in and day out you've got a much bigger problem. If you aren't creating new problems, you aren't moving. If you aren't moving, you aren't progressing.

Both guppies and sharks can have "money problems." For example, a guppy's money problem might be how to afford rent this month. A shark's money problem might be wondering how to reinvest the thousands of dollars he just made on a property sale. Both problems have to do with money, but they're completely different. Which would you rather have?

Change the way you view problems. Instead of thinking of new problems as a negative thing, seek them out. New problems mean you are growing. The only way to get new problems is to take action. Instead of worrying that action will cause problems, know that it will! And that is a good thing.

The key is to keep moving. Nike had it right: "Just Do It!"

BOTTOM LINE: Get in the game, and stay in the game. Become a member of the CIA—take consistent imperfect action. Done is better than perfect. Instead of worrying about problems, know that creating new problems is a good thing. Just do it.

For bonus material on getting yourself to take action, go to TheFishOutOfWaterBook.com/CIA

CHAPTER 2

THE POWER OF DECISION

Eric Worre is the most watched, trusted, and influential person in the entire network marketing profession. He's the author of the bestselling book on network marketing called "Go Pro," and he created the platform Network Marketing Pro, which is the largest resource the network marketing industry has ever known. His events attract thousands and thousands of people from hundreds of different network marketing companies from all over the world. In short, Eric is a shark.

This isn't a book on network marketing, so what does Eric Worre have to do with you being a *fish out of water*? It's this—even though Eric Worre is widely known for his success in the network marketing profession, what is less known is his struggle early on.

Eric Worre wasn't always successful. He started out as a *fish out of water* just like you and me. He struggled getting started in the network marketing profession. Not just for a few days or weeks either! Year after year and company after company Eric struggled!

Then, it all changed. After four years of failure, in a single moment, something finally clicked. After all those years of heartache, suffering, and jumping from company to company, Eric focused on something that he talks about today as "the one thing if there ever was one thing" that got him on the path to his success—the path to becoming a shark. That one thing was: **a decision.**

You already made the decision.

Eric had made a decision to be in network marketing. But, while he was in his struggle, he wasn't serious about it. There was always the option of going back to what was comfortable. He hadn't really committed to his decision.

It wasn't until that moment four years into his career that everything changed. It was in that moment that Eric realized that he had already made the decision, so now he was going to start acting like it! That meant that his focus would adjust from *short-term* thinking to *long-term* thinking. Network marketing wasn't something he was going to "try out." This was something he was committed to becoming an expert in. He was going to go pro.

Just like Eric, committing to the decision you made is where everything changes. Realizing you made a decision gives you power. It gives you clarity and focus. The reason you're a *fish out of water* in the first place is because you decided to level up. You decided that you no longer wanted to live in mediocrity. You decided you weren't going to be a guppy and you're going to become a shark. There is no going back to the safe, calm waters in the fishbowl of average. There's no more looking around or chasing "new opportunities."

Decision cuts off all the other roads and distractions. I love the Spanish conquistador story that illustrates the power showing you're serious about your decision. In the early 1500s, a Spanish conquistador and his men landed on an island to overtake it. The incredible thing about this undertaking is, for 600 years, other conquerors with far more resources and manpower attempted to take control of the same island, and no one ever succeeded. But this time, these conquerors had one vision in mind—take the island. The conquistador gave an order to his men that proved to be the winning factor: **burn the boats!** There was no turning back. Burning the boats showed they were serious. They were there to overtake the island and overtake the island they did.

That's what decisions do. Decisions are burning the boats. The great news is, energy is no longer wasted and instead comes to one focal point—to the most important thing right in front of you. The worst thing a *fish out of water* can do is forget they made a decision. You made a decision to level up. That was your first step to progress. Stay the course no matter what.

Make a decision and *then* make it right.

Something that can hold you back is worrying about the decision you already made. What if you end up making the *wrong* decision? This was a huge problem for me!

As a new entrepreneur, I often found myself lost, confused, and overwhelmed. There are always many choices to be made—what business to get into, what business model to go with, what domain name to buy, how often to post on social media, and the list goes on and on! Often times, I would take *forever* to make a decision. What's worse is after making the decision I would constantly second guess myself, wondering if I made the *right* decision. "Maybe I should have gone with blue instead of red for that logo?" "Maybe I should have signed up for CrossFit instead of buying a Gold's Gym membership."

All the worries were enough to constantly feel uneasy at best, and wake up in a cold sweat in the middle of the night at worst. One day, I was having a conversation with my business coach and mentor, Nick Unsworth. I told Nick what was going on. I felt like I had so much on my plate. Not only did I have a boatload of decisions to make, but what if I messed up? What if I made the *wrong* decision? What would happen?

"Calvin," Nick said intently, "sharks don't worry if they made the right decision or not."

Well, yeah, of course, *they* don't! That must be why they are sharks, I thought. That's why they are successful. They must have some gift of always knowing what the right decision is! That way they never have to worry or revisit the same decision again!

Then, Nick went on to explain that successful people are human just like him and me. Successful people just have a different way of viewing decisions that is completely different from most people. What Nick said next changed my life forever. "Calvin you have it wrong. **Instead of worrying if they made the right decision, successful people make a decision *and then they make it right.*"**

Whoa! That hit me like a ton of bricks! In other words, it's not the point if it's the "right" decision. The decision is just the beginning that gets things moving. It's the *commitment* to the decision and the energies that you put into the decision *after* it's made that makes it a right or wrong decision in the end.

You see, whether a decision was right or wrong is only known in hindsight—not when the decision is actually made. Successful people *make* the decision *right* by putting focus, energy, and attention to the decision. They are in control of making it right or wrong by how they spend their time and energy *after* the decision is made.

Eric Worre had made a decision to be a professional in a particular industry. At first, he wasn't serious about the decision. Then after four years of struggle, he realized he made the decision and he would do everything he could to make that decision right. He would attend the best events. He would educate himself on the best practices. And most importantly, he would take the best actions he knew even though they didn't feel natural at first. That ultimately is what would give him the success he enjoys today.

It's not the time the decision is made that makes it right or wrong. Imagine for a moment that a man and a woman get married. That's a decision. Suppose that the man worries and wonders if he made the right decision or not. What would happen? He would constantly look at other women and think "hmm...maybe I should have married *her* instead." Over time, he would look at his wife and be critical with the things that she does. What do you think would be the inevitable outcome of this relationship? It would be sour at best, and would likely fall apart in the end.

Now imagine that the man started out with a completely different view. Suppose that instead of worrying and wondering about the decision, the man realizes he made the decision to marry this woman, so he's going to make it right. Since he chose to make it the right decision, he puts his energy, focus and affections towards her. He's not focused on other "opportunities." He notices all the things about her that validate that he made a *right* decision. The relationship naturally flourishes.

What's important about this analogy is this: the decision in each situation was the same. It's not the decision that will ultimately bring you success or failure—It's how you respond after the decision is made. When you make a decision, don't worry if you made the right one or not. That's wasted energy. Worrying about a decision you already made is a sure way to put you back to being a guppy living in the fishbowl of mediocrity. When you free yourself from the worry of making the right decision, you can make decisions quickly and get moving. Instead, take the decision you made to level up your life and make it right!

Focus on your next chess move.

Life is more like playing a chess game and less like building a house. When it comes to building a structure, you can plan it out step by step, beginning to end. All the pieces and variables are fixed. But you cannot, on the other hand, plan out every step and move that it takes to win the game of chess. Why? Because you have an opponent. That opponent can do things you didn't have planned. As I mentioned earlier, it's unpredictable.

Sometimes as a *fish out of water*, we just wish we knew every step to get to where it is we want to go. We can feel compelled to plan and analyze. But just like you can't plan every move to win in a game of chess, you can't plan every move it's going to take to become a shark.

Let me ask you a question. How many letters are there in life? You might answer 26. If you answered 26 you actually answered incorrectly. Of course, it's a trick question.

There are 26 letters in the *alphabet*, but in *life* the answer is only three.

I'll explain. The only letters are A, B, and Z. "A" represents where you are now. "B" represents the next move. And "Z" represents your ultimate goal of where you want to end up. This is what life is like. It's fairly easy to see where you are (A). You could even have a pretty good guess of what the next step is (B), and you know where you ultimately want to end up (Z). But everything between B-Z is unknown! You don't know the other factors! Guess what? That's okay.

By the way, the "Z" is what most other books teach—how to set goals and create a vision. That's all well and good. In fact, that's what caused you to become a *fish out of water* in the first place. You couldn't have begun without some sort of vision to where you wanted to end up. But what isn't taught is what happens between B-Z—the unknown. As I mentioned in the last chapter, planning is not only a waste of time but all too often very impractical. It's okay to *not* know everything—because, in fact, you can't!

Admittedly, Eric Worre didn't always know what he was doing. But he saw where he was, and made his next best guess. That was enough. *Your* next best guess is enough, too. It's enough because that's all there is. Trying to do anything beyond that is just getting further away from reality, and creates delusion.

BOTTOM LINE: Instead of worrying if you made the right decision or not, make a decision and then make it right! Know where you want to go. See where you are now, and take your next best guess to move forward.

For bonus material on this chapter, go to TheFishOutOfWaterBook.com/Decision

CHAPTER 3

PLAY TO WIN

John Lee Dumas started a podcast in 2012 called *Entrepreneur On Fire*. Podcasting was new to many people at the time, and what was even more novel was John's idea— to have a podcast where a new episode would be released every single day, seven days a week.

The idea started while John was doing a lot of commuting. His trips were often 30 minutes or so, and he could listen to an entire podcast episode while driving. But, something bothered him. He could not find a single business podcast that released a brand new episode every day. John decided to fill that gap.

"You're crazy!" friends warned John. "Nobody will want to listen to a new episode every day! And besides, it's not practical! You have no idea what it's like to record even *one* podcast episode. Let alone every single day seven days a week. If you try to do a new one each and every day, you'll burn out!" John listened, but he went forward anyway.

Just as people warned him, it wasn't as easy as he thought. There was a lot of trial and error. It was a tough start. But because he committed to releasing an episode every day it forced him to get creative. Before long, John figured out how to *batch* the interviews so they were all recorded in one day, and then scheduled out in the days ahead. That helped tremendously to not being threatened by burnout. The impossible "podcast episode every day" idea looked like it might be quite possible after all.

This new podcast wasn't something John was just "going to try out" for a little while. He committed to it. Truth be told, he was going to focus on it until it was successful. He didn't start making money right away, but he kept on moving anyway. Admittedly, he now says, he wasn't even very good at interviewing, at first. He hadn't podcasted before. It was new for him! He felt like a *fish out of water*. But ultimately, things started to work because of one thing: **John played to win.**

John didn't limit himself to short-term thinking. He was in it for the long game. John would podcast over, and over, and over again. To most, what he was doing would seem-numbingly boring. But John believed in the mission and he knew that it would eventually pay off. And pay off it did!

John didn't start monetizing until the better part of a year. He just kept working at it consistently—day in, and day out. After consistently releasing a new episode each and every day, *Entrepreneur On Fire* not only reached the top spot on iTunes' New and Noteworthy, but it was awarded the top business podcast for all of 2013. Today, John Lee Dumas and his crazy podcast idea grosses around $300k each and every month. Not too shabby.

Win in the long game.

One of the quickest ways to reverting back to the fishbowl of mediocrity is by focusing on the short game. Saying you're just going to "try this out for a little while," is a quick road to failure and disappointment. We talked about this in the last chapter on decisions. You have to commit to your decision. Decide, *then* make it right. But what's also important besides making the decision is how long you choose to stay with it. Some people set targets that, if they don't hit, they're going to quit. What inevitably happens is they get discouraged and go back to what they're used to.

To become a shark, your entire focus has to be on what entrepreneur Gary Vaynerchuk calls, "the long game." The long game is shifting your view of doing something for the short term, and doing it for the long term. Instead of thinking about a project being just a few weeks, you shift your thinking in terms of five, ten, fifteen, or even thirty years! Intimidating? It doesn't have to be. What it does though is put you in the right frame of mind for the success you're after.

It changes your focus from doing *what it takes* to be successful, to doing *whatever it takes* to be successful. In other words, it's not just about doing the steps. Sometimes the steps forward are fuzzy or unknown. Instead, it's about committing to keep on moving forward no matter what!

If John Lee Dumas would have focused on the short game, he might have quit podcasting after a few short weeks. "I had no idea what I was getting into," he said. "I hit into problems I couldn't have predicted." But because he decided he was in it for the long game, he kept going. After doing it over, and over, and over, it gained momentum and turned into something special.

When you are in it for the long game, you play differently. You don't get so upset over any short term "setbacks." Your "tragedies" turn into small little bumps along the way. Your losses become stepping-stones on your path to success. You gain perspective. Being in it for the long game is where you develop the courage to believe you will win no matter what. As the saying goes, "It's hard to beat someone who never gives up." – Babe Ruth

Sharks are masters of the mundane.

When you're a *fish out of water*, you're not doing something flashy and sexy every day. As a matter of fact, it's often quite the opposite. One of the most exciting things to me about sharks is knowing this: they didn't get that way from doing something so difficult and unattainable to everyday normal people. Said in a different way, successful people become successful simply because they do things over and over that most other people won't do.

John Lee Dumas has a format for *Entrepreneur On Fire* that's pretty clear-cut. The episode lengths are virtually the same. The flow of the show is reliably predictable. For John, he does much of the same thing continuously. For some, this sounds boring and they quit. But it's John's ability to stay consistent that gives him the success he has.

As mentioned in Jeff Olson's book *The Slight Edge*, Sharks become successful because they are *masters of the mundane*. Successful people do things that, to most people, look very boring. And guess what, they *are* boring! But successful people do them anyway—over, and over, and over again. Winston Churchill said, "success is going from failure to failure without losing enthusiasm." That's true. What's also true, is being able to do the same unsexy things day in and day out to get the needle moving without losing enthusiasm.

Becoming a master of the mundane is how John became a shark in podcasting. Guppies do seemingly ordinary work, get bored, and quit. Sharks, on the other hand, do ordinary work, and then do it again. They do *extra* of the *ordinary*, and that, in the end, is what makes them *extraordinary*.

Success requires a little bit of insanity.

They say that the definition of insanity is doing the same thing over and over, and expecting a different result. Well, I have news for you. When you are a *fish out of water*, you have to be a little insane. A little insanity is what's going to transform you into a shark. When you choose to level up your life, it doesn't happen in an instant. You have to be a little insane because you really will do the same thing over and over, and expect a different result. There is no such thing as overnight success. Instead, you have to keep on grinding at your craft every day, believing that a better result will come from it. So when someone calls you crazy you can smile and agree—knowing that a little insanity is what's going to get you there.

If John wouldn't have had patience, he would have quit early in his journey. Entrepreneurs everywhere would have missed out on one of the best shows in all of podcasting and John wouldn't be enjoying the life he's been able to create. Know this: everything will not click right away and that's okay. But keep moving anyway. Keep going.

Before long, things *will* click, and you will get into the flow of your life. You'll be well on your way to becoming a shark. Patience is the game.

BOTTOM LINE: Be in it for the long game—do whatever it takes. Sharks are masters of the mundane. Become extraordinary by doing *extra* of the *ordinary*. Be a little insane—do the same thing over and over and expect a different result.

For bonus material on this chapter, go to TheFishOutOfWaterBook.com/PlayToWin

SECTION 2

GET SCHOOLED

IN SECTION 1, WE TALKED ABOUT THE FIRST KEY TO BECOMING A SHARK WHEN YOU'RE A *FISH OUT OF WATER*— CONSISTENT IMPERFECT ACTION.

IN THIS SECTION, WE'LL TALK ABOUT THE SECRETS TO ACCELERATING YOUR SUCCESS IN LEVELING UP YOUR LIFE FASTER THAN EVER BEFORE. YOU DO THAT BY GETTING SCHOOLED!

CHAPTER 4

GET AROUND OTHER FISH OUT OF WATER

When I quit my day job to embark on my journey of being a fulltime entrepreneur, it felt exhilarating! I knew it was the right thing to do! I felt great! Then, one day passed. Quitting my job quickly became the most frightening thing I've ever done in my entire life. I only knew that I did not want to be an employee anymore and that's what got me to get moving. To say I had anxiety, worry, and stress would be massive understatements. I thought, "Now that I am my own boss, what do I do next?" As *fish out of water*, I felt like I could barely breathe. In fact, at times, I felt like I might be suffocating.

But I "burned the boats" and didn't want to be tempted to go back to being a guppy. I decided to do something to challenge myself even more, so I moved from Utah to Southern California and started working for myself selling solar door-to-door. But while I was doing door-to-door sales and had the freedom that came from that, I was still under massive stress. What could I do for my own business? How does this entrepreneur thing work?

Early one morning, shortly after my move to Southern California, I was on my laptop watching YouTube videos from different entrepreneurs. I happened to stumble upon this guy named "Nick Unsworth." After doing a little research, I discovered that Nick, too, lived in Southern California. Also, he had an event coming up in a couple weeks in San Diego. I decided to attend.

At the event, Nick offered an opportunity to do business coaching with him and get connected with other people in the program through masterminds and get-togethers. I decided to take Nick up on his offer. Because I became a part of different masterminds, I was privileged to connect with other entrepreneurs just like me for the first time— creating a business of their own. These people have become my closest friends. Many of them feel like family. For the first time, I was around people who finally "get me."

One of the biggest mistakes a *fish out of water* can make is going at it alone. You might get excited for this new life that you're leveling up to, and then get on trekking. (Which is good because you should get in the game and start taking action.) But here's the truth that isn't talked about enough—*nobody makes it alone*.

When you make it, it will be because of the help of others. It will be because you surrounded yourself with other people like you and other people better than you. It will be because you learned from someone ahead of you. You stood on the shoulders of giants. It will be because you "got schooled." A school, in fish terms, is a group of fish that swim in the same direction. That is your aim—to surround yourself with other people moving in the same direction as you.

You are the average of the five people you spend the most time with.

One of the most detrimental things you can do when you are aiming higher in life is not changing your circle of influence—the people you spend time with. Chances are, even your current friends and family may not be going after the same things you are. It's actually very rare to want to become a shark. It's nothing against your loved ones. But you need to know the truth. The way to get through the *fish out of water* stage and create a new standard for yourself is to surround yourself with other *fish out of water* just like you. Jim Rohn said, "You are the average of the five people you spend the most time with." Make certain those people are the people you *want* to be like.

Whether you realize it or not, spending time with the wrong set of people can put invisible chains on you that you don't even know about. If you hang out with five unhealthy people, chances are you will be the sixth. If you hang out with five broke people, chances are you will be the sixth. But the great news is, if you hang out with five people crushing it in business, chances are you will be the sixth.

Find other people who are interested in the same goals and dreams as you are, and get around them. Become part of the community that they too are a part of. This is why

Crossfit is so successful. People love it. If you ask Crossfitters the number one reason they love it, the answer is always the same—"the people." It's because it's a community of likeminded people moving in the same direction. It's a group of dedicated people, going after similar goals, who understand you, and support you. It's its own unique culture.

The magic from other *fish out of water.*

There are a number of benefits that come from surrounding yourself with other *fish out of water* just like you. Two major advantages are *support* and *speed.* First off, being a *fish out of water* is no easy business. You're getting outside of your comfort zone. It's awkward. It feels weird. You feel like you're gasping for air. You flounder. Some days it's all you can do to not revert back to what you're comfortable with. You're facing new challenges every day. But when you get around other people who are stretching themselves just like you are, they "get" you, and they inspire you. You motivate each other. It gives you the understanding and support you need to keep going.

The other major advantage is the *speed* at which you learn. Even though you're going after similar things as the other *fish out of water*, your experiences are still going to vary. Because they vary, you're able to learn from one another. You get to see your blind spots. You're able to discover things from different angles from other people. Your mistakes will help someone else avoid that pitfall and vice versa.

For example, I was talking with one of my good friends Jenn who had done social media agency work before, and I was barely getting started in that industry. She was able to give me some hugely valuable tips on how to get started the right way—how to structure contracts, etc. By the same token, she wondered how to gain credibility that comes from being published with a recognizable name. Because I had recently been featured in popular blogs like Entrepreneur Magazine and The Huffington Post, I was able to help Jenn save time by sharing the path I followed to get published.

The support you have from your peers who are in the game with you is invaluable. It's important to reemphasize here that I'm not talking about getting around just any person that can give you support. (Even though there are professions for that.) It's getting around the *right* people. People who are *fish out of water* just like you, going after similar goals and dreams.

Yes, you can learn from anyone. But, if you surround yourself with the wrong crowd you can find yourself in a group of guppies. Nothing will tear you down faster. And yes, sometimes it can even be a family member. So instead of getting around just anybody, get around those who are going after it, too. Those are the ones who will understand you and will be on the same page as you. That's where the magic starts to happen.

What you believe is what you will achieve.

A mentor once told me that what separates a millionaire from a lower income earner is one thing—belief. *Some believe they can, so they do, while others believe they can't, so they don't.* As Napoleon Hill says in his classic book, *Think and Grow Rich,* "Whatever the mind can conceive and believe it can achieve."

When you're leveling up some part of your life, you are going against the tide big time! It's not the "norm" to be outstanding. It's very easy to get in spaces of doubt and uncertainty. As a dreamer, we are also our own worst critic. Since we want things to be perfect and they inevitably don't turn out perfect, we start to wonder what we are really capable of. We question what we really can achieve.

One of the biggest boosts to your belief and confidence is being around people who are going after what you're going after. Prior to the 1950s, runners wondered if it was possible for a human being to run a four-minute mile. Many attempted it, and all failed. It became an acceptable "fact" that it was impossible for any human to run a four-minute mile. Then in 1954, a runner named Roger Bannister achieved the first four-minute mile. This shocked the whole world! The impossible was now possible.

Roger Bannister is well known for being the first person to break the four-minute barrier. What isn't as well known is that Roger Bannister's record only lasted 46 days! You see, when people saw what was possible everything changed. For years no one had achieved it and so everyone just accepted that it was impossible. But because someone now did it, runners knew it was possible. Hundreds and hundreds of people have achieved it since.

This is why it's critical to be around other outstanding players because it will increase your belief in what's possible. Sometimes when you don't see it, it's hard to believe it. If we don't have someone to lean on, it can make going through the process of becoming a shark nearly impossible. That's the importance of getting around other *fish out of water*. When you see others going after the same things you are, you're inspired. You start to think, "hey, if they can do it, I can do it."

Increasing that belief level is what will get you up in the morning to take new actions, and have the confidence that *you* can actually succeed. As the Henry Ford quote goes: "whether you think you can or think you can't, you're right." Find a group of people like you. Look on Meetup.com. Join a club. Find a business mastermind. Attend events. The most important thing is to find a group of like-minded people who are dedicated and going after similar goals and dreams like you.

BOTTOM LINE: Get around other fish out of water—people who are leveling up their lives in a similar way to you. That will give you the support, inspiration, and belief you need to keep moving upward.

For bonus material on this chapter, go to TheFishOutOfWaterBook.com/OtherFish

CHAPTER 5

SURROUND YOURSELF WITH SHARKS

Lewis Howes is a super successful online businessman, host of the *School of Greatness* podcast, and author of the best-selling book, *The School of Greatness*. He's in high demand and is often asked to speak at conferences and events at premium prices all over the world. Lewis is a shark.

But he didn't start out that way. In 2006, no one had a clue who Lewis Howes was. In fact, he wasn't sure *he* knew who he was anymore. Lewis had been pursuing his dream of playing pro sports in arena football. Two games into the regular season, he dove for a football and collided into a wall, breaking his wrist. Ouch! Ultimately, in just one season, the injury made it impossible for Lewis to return to the sport he loved. Just like that, Lewis's entire football career was over.

Now what? At the end of the season, Lewis underwent surgery that would take some time to recover. With no money, he ended up moving in with his sister and sleeping on her couch. Feeling broken, in more ways than one, Lewis had to find a new dream. He had to reinvent himself.

Lewis had the heart of a champion with tremendous drive to succeed. He just didn't know where to start. But he realized that he needed to get moving if he was going to make a name for himself. He began networking and going to different events in his Ohio hometown. He eventually got connected with different business people and mentors. One of his mentors advised him to check out LinkedIn to find a job.

He took that advice and started looking into the professional social networking site, LinkedIn. With nothing better to do besides sit on his sister's coach in a big cast, Lewis explored LinkedIn for hours and hours every day. Instead of looking at LinkedIn as a place to find a job, though, he explored all the possibilities LinkedIn had to offer. Lewis became nothing short of a LinkedIn expert and started hosting small events at restaurants to teach people about LinkedIn. He was establishing himself in the online business space.

After a while, Lewis moved from Ohio to New York and connected with other top names in the online business world, like Marie Forleo, Derek Halpern, and Ramit Sethi. Another person Lewis had connected with, Joel Comm, invited Lewis onto a webinar to talk about LinkedIn. Lewis was able to sell a boot camp at the end of the webinar. After that webinar, Lewis saw more money in his PayPal account than he ever imagined. He was hooked, and this was just the beginning.

Lewis Howes started out how we all do. He had a huge desire to level up in his life. But when he started, he knew exactly *zero* people in the online space. He was *a fish out of water*. He took boatloads of action, and then Lewis also did the next step that was essential to becoming the shark that he is today. Lewis "got schooled."

Not only did Lewis surround himself with other people who were in the game as well, he also connected with sharks. He found mentors. He offered value to them and received advice and value in return. Those mentors would prove to be a huge acceleration in Lewis's success. Lewis didn't know what the online space was like. He didn't know the level of opportunities it had for him. But because he surrounded himself with mentors who were already playing the game, he put himself in a position to win.

In addition to getting around other *fish out of water* who are in the same game as you, get with some sharks. Sharks are already where you want to be. They are *proof* that you can succeed because they're already there. I've been fortunate to find myself in the company of sharks in different chapters of my life. They offer a vision of what's possible and give you a model to go after.

If I have seen further, it is by standing on the shoulders of giants. -Isaac Newton

As a floundering *fish out of water*, there is nothing that can give you a deep breath of fresh air like mentor can. A mentor is someone who has already walked the walk, and can guide you on your path as well. It's valuable to surround yourself with other people playing the game, but what's also essential is getting around people who are either ahead of you, or who have already finished the game.

They know the pitfalls to avoid. They know what strategies worked for them, and which ones didn't. The best part about mentors is after they've achieved the level of success they have, they almost feel this *duty* to share what they've learned. So it doesn't take much effort to find a mentor who is willing to share their wisdom.

It will take sacrifice on your part to get the most out of a mentor. Instead of saying "can I take you out to lunch and pick your brain," Lewis asked his mentors how he could provide value to them. He also showed seriousness and sacrifice by moving from Ohio to New York to get around more mentors.

In addition to getting a mentor in person, you can find them in other forms as well. You can find mentors in books. Robert Kiyosaki, for example, I mentioned wrote the book *Rich Dad, Poor Dad*. Through that book, Robert Kiyosaki has mentored me, and I haven't even met him in real life (yet). Dave Ramsey is another mentor of mine through his book *Total Money Makeover*. Tony Robbins has mentored me through his countless videos and audio programs. You can get information from the mentor in many forms. What's important is that you find someone who has knowledge, experience and passion about the things you want to know about.

Attend events.

I haven't used the word "hack" in this book yet. But if there's a "hack" to getting around other sharks, it's this—attend events. Going to different business and entrepreneurship events is what has allowed me to meet sharks like Robert Herjavec and Daymond John (pun intended—since they're both from the hit TV show, Shark Tank).

Events are where I've been blessed to be around other entrepreneurs I admire, like Gary Vaynerchuk, Grant Cardone, Tai Lopez, Brendon Burchard, Russell Brunson, Sean Stevenson and many more. All of these people I first discovered from afar, then was able to connect with them on a deeper level in person at an event. When you attend enough events you start to see how real, and normal these people are. It gives you an opportunity to provide value to them, and develop a relationship. That relationship is worth more than money. It's what will help *you* become a shark.

If you're aiming to level up your life, there's nothing like attending events. Events are not only designed to give you breakthrough information, but they are swimming with sharks! Getting some sharks to look to will give you the example to model your behavior and actions on to achieve the life you want.

Invest in a coach.

In Spring 2016, Carrie Dickie was named "One of the Most Powerful Women in Network Marketing" on none other than Eric Worre's stage. Carrie was also featured and interviewed by Grant Cardone as a "Network Marketing Mogul." In the same year, she released her first book *Network Marketing: The View from Venus,* which quickly became a #1 Amazon bestseller. Carrie is a shark.

But like all other sharks, she wasn't always that way. Throughout most of Carrie's life, she was unhappy, scared, and anxious. She considered herself unworthy and was full of self-doubt. This wasn't just when she was a

teenager either. This lasted up into her late
40s! At an age where many people might
settle and say "well, I guess this is it," Carrie
decided to take control of her life. In 2008,
Carrie made a decision that would put her on
a path to changing her life forever—Carrie
hired a coach.

Carrie's life coach, Tawny Avonne,
helped Carrie transform her life. For years
Carrie thought everybody had it together
except her. She believed she wasn't enough.
Those beliefs sabotaged every aspect of her
life. But after working with a coach, her
beliefs made a complete shift. Tawny helped
Carrie not only see her potential, but also her
true self—a person who was already perfect,
whole, and complete. Carrie went on to create
one of the most successful network marketing
organizations in the industry, and inspires the
lives of thousands all over the world.

In June 2015, I did something similar—at
the time it was one of the scariest things I had
ever done in my life. At Nick Unsworth's
event in San Diego, I hired him to be my
business coach. The commitment? $20,000.
For me, the equivalent of buying more than
two cars! I had never invested in anything that
size in my entire life! I could barely believe I

did it. But I figured if I really wanted to become a millionaire and achieve the level of success I said I did, I needed to show that I was serious—I would need to be willing to invest in myself.

I used lessons from the last section. I took consistent imperfect action. I had made the decision and now I was determined to make it right. This was one of the scariest things I had ever done, but it was also one of the best things I had ever done. A coach, someone you hire to help you level up in your life, can save you years of heartache!

The highest achievers in the world, like Michael Jordan, had coaches. When your head is down and you're working away, it's easy to miss the details. When you're too close to the situation it's difficult to see what's obvious to a skilled eye on the outside looking in. That's what Carrie's coach helped her do—see her own stuff, work through it, and transform. That's what Nick did for me. A coach is someone who can watch you while you're in the game of life and help you make minor adjustments that make huge differences. Many of these adjustments are blind to you. But a coach's different perspective and experience will help you see those blind spots.

My coach, Nick Unsworth, who graciously wrote the foreword of this book, has helped me shave years of trial and error. His mentor did it for him, and now he's doing it for me. A good coach is better than a success blueprint or roadmap. A good coach is like a success GPS—he or she shows you where you are and gives you turn-by-turn directions depending on where you stand currently and where you want to end up.

I always wanted to be an entrepreneur, but I didn't know the steps to take or how long it would take for it to become a reality. In the first year of working with a coach, I started a couple different businesses (experimenting to find what fit me best), I became featured in top publications like Entrepreneur Magazine, The Huffington Post, and Social Media Examiner, I've started public speaking, and I've grown my social media business.

Accomplishing as much as I have, in the short time it's been, can be attributed to having someone understand what I didn't, guide me, and help me get better. To speed up your process of becoming a shark, do yourself a favor. Do what the sharks do. Get a coach.

By the way, a side benefit of having a good coach is they are likely connected with other sharks as well. It gives you access to a world you might not have even knownb existed. You'll end up finding friends and super high-level players you otherwise wouldn't have had the opportunity to meet.

This is why Lewis Howes became so successful. He not only got in the game and started taking action, but he surrounded himself with movers and shakers. That gave him the power he needed to level up his game and to create a new standard for himself. You can do the same thing for you, too.

BOTTOM LINE: Get around sharks. Mentors and coaches can shave years off your learning curve, and one of the easiest places to connect with them is through events. To really accelerate your learning, hire a coach.

For bonus material on this chapter, go to TheFishOutOfWaterBook.com/Sharks

CHAPTER 6

ACCOUNTABILITY

Gary Vaynerchuk is one of my personal heroes. As a child, he immigrated to the United States with his parents from the former Soviet Union. He's a total entrepreneur through and through. When delivering his keynotes, he'll often recall times as a young kid where he would pick flowers from his neighbor's yards and sell it back to them! Talk about hustle. He's also not afraid to drop the F-bomb in a large crowd, which I also appreciate.

Like most young entrepreneurs, he also had the lemonade stand business. But instead of just one lemonade stand, he recruited his friends to help him and he had several going at once. At other times in his young life, he would sell baseball cards on the weekend and make a small fortune. One of the reasons I love Gary Vaynerchuk (or "GaryVee" as he's also known) is because he's so real and raw. He didn't do perfectly in school.

What's funny, is after a weekend of selling baseball cards, he would go back to school on Monday only to get scolded by his teachers for his bad grades. "You'll never amount to anything!" They would say. The irony is, little Gary made more money on the weekend selling baseball cards than his teachers did for an entire month!

Gary Vaynerchuk continued his entrepreneurial path because that's all he knew. At fourteen years old, he started working at his dad's liquor shop. In his twenties, he took control of his dad's business and helped it grow from $3 million in annual sales to over $60 million. Gary started one of the first video wine blogs on YouTube called WineLibrary. It became a smashing hit and the gateway to land him on shows like Late Night with Conan O'Brien and The Ellen Show.

GaryVee went on to create one of the most successful social media agencies, VaynerMedia, which as of this writing, in summer 2016, has over 600 employees. Gary has a couple popular YouTube shows, #AskGaryVee—where he answers fan questions—and DailyVee—where he documents his life as an entrepreneur. In 2016, he continues the hustle. He started a new sports agency called VaynerSports. He's authored four best-selling books and is in high demand in his speaking career (the last I heard his rate is around $50k for a one hour talk— not bad). Needless to say, GaryVee is a massive success. He knows what he wants, and he gets it. He's a total shark. Everything he puts his mind to he dominates it. Well, *almost* everything.

In his late 30s, Gary decided to take his health more seriously. He'd attempted several times to get into better shape. But he had very little progress. In fact, he struggled—which you might find very surprising. Here's a guy who has accomplished so much. As someone who plans to *own* the New York Jets, he's no small dreamer. He's a shark on so many levels. But even GaryVee was struggling to get his health where he wanted it.

Fast forward to today—GaryVee turns 41 at the end of 2016, and if you look at his videos online, it's clear that he is in the best shape of his entire life. He finally cracked the code. After months and months of hitting the wall, something finally clicked. What changed?

Ultimately, Gary had hired a personal trainer named Mike. Mike was in charge of Gary's overall health. He trained with Gary virtually every day, and he showed Gary exactly what to eat. GaryVee started answering to Mike on almost a daily basis.

The secret to hitting your target.

I recently attended an event where GaryVee was the keynote. It was hard to miss how good of shape he was in! Someone asked Gary about his health. He had struggled for so long and now he looked so good! Something had obviously changed. What made it finally click? How did he suddenly get in the shape he always wanted to? "It boils down to one word," Gary said matter-of-factly, *"accountability."*

Gary went on to explain that in every other area of his life that had been wildly successful, he noticed he had accountability. As a young person working in his dad's liquor store he had accountability to his dad. At VaynerMedia, he had accountability to his employees and clients. Doing the

#AskGaryVee show he had accountability to his fans asking questions.

The one area in his life he didn't have accountability was his health, and that is why it suffered. It wasn't that Gary was lazy. In fact, he made a decision to get healthy and he took steps to get healthy. But by going at it alone, nothing stuck—at least not long-term. As soon as he hired Mike, that gave him the accountability he needed. It was just enough to keep Gary from eating things he shouldn't eat, and working out as consistently as he should. Gary created a new standard.

When you're a *fish out of water* looking to level-up your life, it's easy to "fall off the wagon." The cure is to seek accountability. Using the example of Gary, it's obvious that the best of the best use accountability to their advantage.

Accountability doubles your chances of achieving success.

When you don't have accountability, it's scary how very low your chances of hitting your goals actually are. Even when you're a strong-willed shark like GaryVee it's not easy. But, if you have some way to create accountability, your results skyrocket. In the best-selling book, *The ONE Thing*, author Gary Keller says that people who at least write their goals down on paper are 39.5% more likely to succeed. But, people who get someone to also hold them accountable are 76.7% more likely to achieve success! That's nearly double in effectiveness! This is exactly what GaryVee did. When he hired Mike, he had to report to him almost daily. Having that system of accountability is what helped him get the results in his health that he desired.

As a *fish out of water*, there are action items and tasks that you know you need to do consistently to create the results your after. But sometimes you won't feel like doing them. The key is to find an accountability partner who can meet with you on a regular basis to go over your commitments with yourself. It keeps you honest with yourself. You stay true, to you.

Get accountability from the right people.

It matters who holds you accountable. Be certain you're getting accountability from the right people. Probably said in a better way, be certain you're not getting accountability from the *wrong* people. Just as I mentioned in the last couple of chapters, you want to surround yourself with high-level players. When you aim to achieve something great in life, you want to not only surround yourself with other *fish out of water* and sharks, but these are the kind of people you also want to get accountability from.

Don't get accountability from guppies. Guppies (people who are comfortable living life small) won't understand you. They won't understand why you're aiming as high as you are, and they won't push you. It's critical to get accountability from a peer—another *fish out of water*—or from a shark—someone who's already on the level you are aspiring to. Don't get fitness accountability from a fat person. Don't get financial advice from someone who's broke. Make sure it's someone you would trade places with.

These people will not only understand you better, but they will also push you to be better. In short, take Oprah's advice; "surround yourself with people who are going to lift you higher!" No wildly successful person ever got there on their own. Be smart who you pick as friends. Get schooled. Get around the right people, and create a system of accountability.

BOTTOM LINE: Even the most successful people in the world use accountability. Accountability doubles your chances of success! Get accountability from the right people.

For bonus material on this chapter, go to TheFishOutOfWaterBook.com/

Accountability

SECTION 3

S.W.I.M. LIKE A SHARK

CONGRATULATIONS ON MAKING IT THIS FAR! YOU NOW KNOW THE FIRST TWO PRINCIPLES TO PRACTICE WHEN YOU ARE FLOUDERING AND GASPING FOR AIR—TAKE CONSISTENT IMPERFECT ACTION, AND GET SCHOOLED— SURROUND YOURSELF WITH THE RIGHT PEOPLE. YOU ARE WELL ON YOUR WAY TO BECOMING A SHARK. THE GREAT THING IS, ONCE YOU'RE A SHARK, YOU CAN'T GO BACK. YOU CREATE A NEW STANDARD.

IN THIS LAST SECTION, YOU'LL DISCOVER THE PIECE TO THE PUZZLE THAT HOLDS EVERYTHING TOGETHER. YOU'RE GOING TO LEARN HOW TO SWIM LIKE A SHARK!

SWIM STANDS FOR SUCCESS, WORDS, IMPROVE, AND MEASURE.

CHAPTER 7

SUCCESS – HOW SHARKS DEFINE IT

You know how important it is to take consistent imperfect action, and surround yourself with the right people. Now you'll discover the final piece that holds everything together. You'll learn how to behave like successful people — how to SWIM like a shark. The "S" in "SWIM" stands for "success." Success is something we all think about. It's something we all desire. It's no secret that when you are successful you feel more confident. But how can someone be more in control of their own success and thus be confident more often?

My first mentor, Marion Timpson, would always say, "Calvin, success breeds confidence, and confidence breeds success."

It's a cycle. When we are successful, we feel better about ourselves. When we feel capable, we're more likely to succeed again. After creating success our confidence goes up. The problem is, what if our successes are few and far between? What happens to our confidence then? It's not like success is something we can just call on demand every day. Success is something so hard to achieve consistently. Or is it?

A cheat-code to life.

I used to define success much differently than I do today. I learned that how you define success ultimately determines how much you have confidence in yourself, and how far you will go. Several years back when I was learning how to sell, I was bummed one day looking at the numbers. I had made dramatic improvements since the day I almost got fired. But, I wasn't number one yet. I desperately wanted to be, so I determined I would be. The way to get there was to make more sales. I began to shift my attention away from the customer and put all of my focus and energies onto the most important thing that was success to me—getting more sales! I knew the success I wanted to have, and I was going to get it.

I'm sure the customers could smell what is called "commission breath," because something happened that I was not expecting. With my new determination to get more sales, surely my performance would be on the rise. On the contrary, though, my sales conversion tanked! In a panic, I tried even harder to get sales. Every call that came in I wished and wished it would end in a sale. If it didn't, I was devastated. Before I knew it, I was trailing further, and further behind. I hated how I felt.

One day I decided that the negative feelings I'd been having weren't worth it. I had chosen between taking care of the customer and getting more sales. I wasn't really focused on the customer so I felt bad for that, but I wasn't even getting more sales for it either! Besides, even if I got more sales I wouldn't feel good about myself for neglecting the customer. If my conversion was going to be low, I at least wanted to feel good. I decided to put all of my focus, energy, and attention *not* on getting the sale, but just on taking care of the customer.

Something interesting happened—my sales conversion skyrocketed! What?! How could this be? I couldn't believe it! "Getting sales" wasn't even the goal anymore. How the heck did I get more sales? In the beginning, I thought I had to decide between caring for the customer and caring about getting sales. After putting so much focus on sales, ruining my conversion and feeling how bad I felt, I decided *that* wasn't the thing I wanted to focus on. But now, not only did I feel better because I was no longer neglecting the customer, but my sales conversion went up too! I got both! I was shocked! I thought I discovered a cheat-code to life.

"Do not be concerned with the fruit of your action—just give attention to the action itself. The fruit will come of its own accord." – Eckhart Tolle

What I didn't realize until years later is I had stumbled on a success secret of sharks. The biggest difference between a shark and a guppy is where they place the idea of success. Success to a guppy is *outside* of his control, while success to a shark is *inside* his control. After setting a goal, successful people don't obsess about the result—something outside their control. They put their focus on the action itself—*the things within their control.* That is where success truly lives. You might ask, why is it such a big deal to think of success as doing the action, and not so much hitting the result? Surely, the pro athlete is satisfied when he wins the game. A farmer is proud when he harvests his crop at the end of the season.

That's probably true. There are two important reasons for placing success on the action vs. the result. First, the result happened *because* of the actions that were taken. Without the actions, the results won't happen. You can take actions without getting the desired result, but you can't get the desired result without taking action. Success is largely a choice. You can choose your actions within your control, but you can't choose the result that will come from those actions. As Eckhart Tolle said, "the fruit will come of its own accord." Sharks put their focus on the action because they know that's the path to achieving their goal.

Second, if success didn't come until a result is achieved, you'd be waiting to feel confident, too. And what if the result doesn't happen at all? You'd be putting confidence in the hands of something outside your control. Your feeling of confidence would be at risk, which would slow your momentum.

It's no secret that life isn't always *fixed*. Circumstances often happen differently than we could have predicted. We don't always hit the result in the way and time we thought we should have. Not feeling successful can make us feel down—even down on ourselves! We may begin to doubt ourselves. We wonder if we're really good enough. We feel less confident, less in control. Here's the tragedy—on the next go-round, we might play small. We didn't like how not achieving the result felt, so we aim lower. This is the real danger in thinking success is arriving at the target, rather than taking your best shot.

Let's look at two scenarios. We have Bob and Phil. Both Bob and Phil have a goal to get into better shape and increase their confidence. Bob wants to push himself, but he doesn't want to push himself *too much*. He stretched himself once before where he set a goal and came up short. He didn't feel good about himself after that, so he learned to be more "realistic" with his goal-setting this time around. Bob thinks he's probably capable of running a full marathon, but just to be safe, he aims lower. He signs up for a half marathon instead. After all, he already ran more than 10 miles at one time before, so it's a safe bet.

Phil, like Bob, has also run more than 10 miles before. But Phil wants to *really* push himself. Phil also believes he is capable of running a marathon. But Phil decides to sign up not for a marathon, but for an ultra-marathon — 50 miles.

The weeks leading up to their respective races are very different. Even though they started in the same place, their training varies greatly in intensity. Bob takes it easy. He runs once a week on Saturday for about 30 minutes. Phil on the other hand, trains at least 3 times a week for 45-mins to an hour.

When race-day comes, Bob feels ready for the half-marathon. During the race, he gets winded and only struggles a little bit, but after several hours he finishes the race! On race day for Phil, he's honestly not sure how much he'll be able to complete. But he's been training hard and gives it the best he can. It proves to be the most difficult thing he's ever done. After several hours, he's gone 20 miles — just 6 miles short of a full marathon. At this point, his right knee starts to bother him — but he keeps pushing anyway. He runs until his body finally gives out. He ends up running 37 miles.

The question is, who did better? Who was more successful, Bob or Phil? The answer depends on your definition of success. Based on most people's definition, Bob, the guy who completed the half-marathon is actually more successful than Phil. He set a goal and accomplished it 100%. Phil on the other hand only got to 74% of his goal. So he wasn't as successful, right?

If you want to continue to get better and live life like a shark, it's dangerous to define success like most people. Bob and Phil had the same starting point. Both wanted to get into better shape. The only difference is the arbitrary goal they set for themselves. Bob hit his target. Phil, on the other hand, did not hit his target. But get this: compared to where he started, Phil improved 307% above his starting point! Bob, on the other hand, was 150% better—literally half of Phil's improvement!

Phil set a goal that was high and he wasn't even sure if he could hit it. But it caused him to take massive action. It stretched him. He improved himself several times over.

He took action toward his potential, and he dramatically improved from his starting point.

Sharks focus on the actions, not the result.

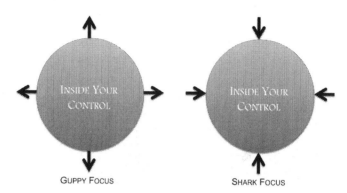

GUPPY FOCUS   SHARK FOCUS

If you take this one key you will be well on your way to the success you desire. Successful people focus *inside* their control while unsuccessful people place their focus *outside* their control. When things don't turn out the way a guppy thinks it should, it's because of something that happened outside of them. So, they blame.

If you listen to great coaches talk to their players, their main focus in not on winning the game—the *result* they're after. Almost all great coaches talk about putting themselves *in a position to win*. In other words, they're focused on themselves doing the right thing and letting the result take care of itself. This is what Eckhart Tolle meant when he said, "Do not be concerned with the fruit of your action—just give attention to the action itself. The fruit will come of its own accord." When you focus on what's in your control, you behave differently. You feel differently. It puts you in control of your own confidence, and your life.

In *The Seven Habits of Highly Effective People,* Stephen Covey shares a major key he discovered when studying the difference between successful and unsuccessful people. He noticed that when unsuccessful people focused outward on things not in their control, *outside* their circle of influence, the things they actually had some control over got smaller. They then began to feel even less confident, less in control, more anxious, and more stressed.

On the other hand, when successful people focused on what *was* in their control, *inside* their circle of influence, the things they could control actually expanded over time! That means the things they actually couldn't do anything about directly, in the beginning, slowly became within their control. Their own personal power and influence literally expanded! To think like a shark, focus where you can actually make an impact. Put your attention on things *inside* your control. Focus on the few things you can actually do something about, and your power will grow, too. You can't control if the prospect buys, but you can give the best presentation ever. You can't control if you'll win the race, but you can train hard and give it your best. You can't control if it rains, but you can bring an umbrella.

True success only lives in the moment.

Remember, to be successful you are not *waiting* for anything. Success isn't something you've done, and it's not something you're looking to in the future. Success happens right here, right now—in the moment. It lives nowhere else.

Success is doing what you *can* with what you *have* in the present. The coolest thing about knowing this is you don't have to wait to be a success. You can choose to be successful immediately. It's not some lofty accomplishment that you have to wait years for. On the contrary, the way to achieve your lofty goals in the future is to be successful *today*. It's always 100% in your control. There's always something you can do inside your control.

Shoot for the moon. Even if you miss, you'll land among the stars. –Les Brown

My early mentor, Marion Timpson, had this golden rule: "Focus on what's in your control and *create success* (take action) with those things. That will give you confidence, and increase your chances of accomplishing things that are currently outside of your control."

So what is success? Success is growth. Success is progress. Success is always within your control. The famous basketball coach, John Wooden, who won 10 NCAA national championships, defined success this way: **"Success is peace of mind, which is a direct result of self-satisfaction in knowing you made the effort to do your best to become the best that you are capable of becoming."**

Success is personal. As a *fish out of water*, never aim smaller for fear of not hitting your goal. Success isn't just in hitting the goal anyway. Success is taking action within your control, and making progress. If you are taking action toward your potential, you are growing, you are successful. Sharks are successful because they aim for the moon. They look to where they want to go, regardless of *how* they are going to get there. They are not afraid to set big goals because they know that success is not something they will have someday. It's within their control. The result may not be entirely in their control, but their effort and actions are. They gain more confidence every time they get up and take another step toward their goal. Shoot for the moon! Take one step forward. Be successful.

BOTTOM LINE: Define success like a shark. Instead of focusing on things outside your control, focus on what's directly within your control. Success is not in the future. It's available only in the here and now. Success is personal. By taking action inside your control you are successful and you build confidence.

For bonus material on this chapter, go to TheFishOutOfWaterBook.com/Success

CHAPTER 8

WORDS – SPEAK LIKE A SHARK

In Spring 2016, I attended an event in Scottsdale, Arizona with some friends. The first day ended super late. It was 2:30 in the morning and I was driving to my Airbnb to catch a few hours of sleep before another early start the next day. The rain was pouring down. Visibility was low. Fortunately, I was only one turn away and we would arrive at our destination.

"Turn Right," said my GPS. I flipped my right blinker on and immediately moved into the right turn lane. Only, there was one little problem. SLAM! POP! SCREECH!

"Holy shit!" I said out loud to my friend Eric.

"I think you blew your tire dude," he said matter-of-factly. As it turned out, the "right turn lane" I merged into wasn't a right turn lane at all. It was a freaking sidewalk! Combining me being tired and it pouring rain, I managed to turn right into the curb, popping my front right tire.

We parked at the Airbnb. I got out and looked at my car to inspect for other possible damage. I didn't see anything else, but sure enough, my tire had a big hole in it and was flat as a pancake.

I went in the house. "Gosh damn it!" I said to my friends in disgust. "I am such an idiot!" I was so pissed. I was pissed at the situation. I was pissed that it was so late. I was pissed that it was raining. Above all, I was pissed at myself. "How did I not see the sidewalk? How could I be such an idiot?"

I then started to worry how this might detract from the rest of the weekend. It was supposed to be a great time with my friends. Day two of the event was starting at 9:00. I wasn't going to be getting enough sleep as it is! And because I was such an idiot, I had to get up even earlier to get the spare tire put on, then I would need to take the car to a mechanic to get a new tire put on. Plus I didn't live in Scottsdale! I didn't know where the tire places were. All of this because I didn't pay attention. I was so embarrassed with myself.

"Calvin," one of my friends asked, "you're okay right?"

"You mean physically?" I replied. "Yes, I'm fine."

"That's what really matters. You're saying some mean things about yourself. If someone was calling one of your friends an 'idiot' or talking to them how you're talking to yourself right now, how would you feel?"

Whoa…that hit me like a ton of bricks. "I haven't thought about that before."

"Your words have power. What you say to yourself matters. You can use words to tell yourself a good story or a bad story. How you feel is not based on what happens, it's based on what you tell yourself."

"Besides," another friend said, "it's only a tire. It needed to be replaced anyway."

Wow. I stood there and really took in what my friends said. I couldn't help but noticed I felt…lighter. I didn't feel bad anymore. I wasn't angry. Was the tire suddenly fixed? No. The situation didn't change at all.

I learned something profound that night. I learned that it wasn't the situation itself that was making me feel down, angry, and upset. Instead, it was the words I used to describe the event to myself that made all the difference. It was the story. It was the meaning I placed on that story. I realized *I* was in control of how I felt by the words I used. The best part was, if I didn't like how I felt, I could change it.

As a side note, when I took the car in the next day, the mechanic told me the brakes were about to go out. "It's a good thing you brought this in here!" he said. It turns out blowing my tire wasn't so bad after all.

Sharks speak differently.

Since that night, I began to notice how successful people speak differently than unsuccessful people. Not only were their words different, but the conversations were completely different as well. A friend and mentor of mine, Michael Bernoff is a neuro-linguistic programming expert. In English, that means he knows about words and communication. He told me about the day he realized that the difference between sharks and guppies was in their words. Michael had been on a beach hanging around a group of people known to be making a moderate living—probably middle class. He was sitting and listening to the conversations. Most of the conversations were about The Kardashians, or what was happening in the news, etc. It was mostly people talking about people.

Michael then got up and walked over to where another party was going on. This party was full millionaires and billionaires. The conversations were totally different. These conversations were discussing businesses they were building, inventions that were being made, and healthy arguments were taking place. In short, successful people were talking about ideas. They weren't talking about events or people. That's when Michael realized the words you speak matter.

If you want to feel certain, use certain, empowering language.

"Kind of. Sort of. Sure. Probably. I guess. We'll see." All of these phrases have one thing in common—to a shark, they're all curse words. Sharks do not use *fluffy* uncertain language. These kinds of words take your power away. Instead of "sort of" or "kind of," it's "yes" or "no." It's "absolutely," not "probably." Have you ever felt down and you don't know why? Check your language. Changing the words you say will dramatic effect your overall wellbeing. Sharks use language that is certain, absolute, and empowering.

It's even more impactful if you're in a position of influence. People look to you for leadership. They can't follow someone who seems unsure of where he or she is going. Using certain, empowering language is the key to being persuasive. Tony Robbins says, "When two people meet, the one who is most certain will always influence the other person."

When I decided to change my "fluffy" language to be much more certain and absolute, I enrolled my wife Bekah to hold me accountable. She had permission to call me out every time she heard me speak using "uncertain" language. It's made a massive difference.

It's crazy how disempowering I would speak! Before, I would always worry about being correct or not, so I would speak in a "fluffy" way so I couldn't be wrong. When

Bekah would ask, "are you going to have a good day?" I used to reply, "well, it depends. I don't know yet. I hope so. We'll see." I didn't want to be wrong! Since learning that sharks speak with certainty, the answer is, "yes. Absolutely."

In your transformation to becoming a shark, notice your language and the language of successful people around you. Cut out the fluffy, uncertain words to phrases that are concrete. It might feel awkward at first, as though you're learning a new language. That's because, well, you are. If you want to feel powerful, certain, and strong, use that kind of language.

BOTTOM LINE: Words are power. The stories you tell yourself will determine how you feel. It's not the situation, but what you tell yourself about the situation that matters. Words that successful people speak are certain, absolute, and empowering.

For bonus material on this chapter, go to TheFishOutOfWaterBook.com/Words

CHAPTER 9

IMPROVE – THE KEY TO GROWTH AND HAPPINESS

Tony Robbins is the most successful coach, trainer, and personal transformation specialist in the entire world. He's more than a motivational speaker. Tony is known for taking people with seemingly impossible-to-overcome problems and literally transforming their lives. Tony went from teaching people in small hotel rooms to packing entire stadiums. He's worked with literally millions of people from over one hundred countries all around the world, from small town farmers to high-performing athletes, to leaders of nations. Tony gets results. Tony is a shark.

How is Tony so successful? If you look at Tony today, heck, even the past couple of decades, you might think that he's always been wildly successful. Maybe his parents were rich. Maybe he went to the best schools. He must have had advantages that many of us just didn't have.

None of those are true. On the contrary, what's not as well known as Tony's success is that his family life was far from rich. He actually lived in poverty. His parents got divorced when he was only seven years old. Young Tony was devastated. His parents' divorce led him to being separated from his mom and two younger siblings before he returned to live with his mom at nine years old. His mom was extremely unstable. She went through a number of different husbands and began abusing drugs and alcohol. Tony had anything but a solid adult role model to look up. At a very young age, being the oldest child, Tony became a caregiver for his two younger siblings.

Life for Tony was far from ideal. He recalls going to the store to shop for the family and sometimes stealing food. The "grand" wishes his mother had for him was to become a truck driver because then he could earn a whopping $20,000 per year. His potential didn't look all too bright. In his teenage years, his relationship with his mom grew more distant and rocky. On Christmas Eve when Tony was only 17 years old, he ran away from home. Tony was homeless.

"Life is so unfair," he thought! He had been dealt a bad set of cards. Tony didn't have a solid father figure in his life. His mother was unstable. His growing up years were filled with pain. Now, at just 17 years old, he was homeless and estranged from his own mother.

After Tony Robbins left home and was now living on his own, he ended up working for a man who would become his mentor. This man was a gentleman by the name of Jim Rohn. Jim Rohn was a personal development trainer. One day, Jim Rohn told Tony a simple idea that would change his life forever. "Tony," he said warmly, "if you want more you have to *become* more. For things to change *you* have to change. For things to get better, *you* have to get better. For things to improve *you* have to improve. If *you* grow, everything grows for you."

Up to this point in young Tony Robbins' life, he had placed blame for his poor circumstances on other people around him — on things outside his control. Now, though, he learned that he was responsible for his own destiny. If he wanted a great life it was nobody's responsibility but his. He was in control. Tony took the advice his mentor taught him and made it his mission to make himself better. He committed to continuous personal improvement. The rest is history.

As Tony's new discovery of self-improvement made dramatic differences in his life, it became his purpose to share what he learned with other people—to help them reach their personal peak performance. In the book *Think and Grow Rich*, Napoleon Hill says over and over, "what the mind can conceive and believe, it can achieve." The mind is our most powerful tool. How well you take care of your mind and the mindset you develop will determine how far you will go. Continual, personal improvement is like exercise for the mind. Sharks have discovered this. That's why they make it their business to take care of themselves, expand their mind, and continually improve.

Sharpen the saw.

In *Seven Habits of Highly Effective People*, Stephen Covey talks about the 7th habit of successful people that he calls "sharpen the saw." He noticed this peculiar habit among top performers. It's what Tony Robbins did to turn his life around. It's what he has taught millions of people all around the world. Continual growth, joy, satisfaction and happiness come through continual personal improvement.

Successful people are constantly improving themselves. They're always challenging their comfort zone, and what they know. Guppies remain where they are in the fishbowl of average because they stop learning. They stop improving. The secret is, sharks really never "arrive." They didn't stop learning when they got out of school.

As a *fish out of water,* the key that will unlock your unlimited potential is continual improvement. It's like good compound interest that will pay *you* over, and over, and over again. The momentum of growth you create will begin to take on a life of it's own. Some argue that progress and growth are not only a trait of high achievers but also an actual human need. We crave it and get satisfaction from it. If you're not growing, you're dying. Always looking for ways to stretch your comfort zone and get better is your path to growth.

Continue to sharpen your saw. Read good books. Attend seminars. Take courses or classes that make you better. If you're feeling really adventurous, try new things you've always wanted to do. Watch something like *The Tim Ferriss Experiment* on iTunes for ideas. Go to new places you've always wanted to go. As Jim Rohn said, "For things to change, *you* have to change. For things to get better, *you* have to get better." Continually improve.

BOTTOM LINE: The most successful people in the world continually improve themselves. Look for different ways to consistently get better. Never "arrive." Sharpen your saw.

For bonus material on this chapter, go to TheFishOutOfWaterBook.com/Improve

CHAPTER 10

MEASURE – SHARKS WIN BY KEEPING SCORE

You can't win if you aren't keeping score.

Jerry Seinfeld is one of the most successful comedians of all time. Not only was he wildly successful as a stand-up comedian, but also the sitcom bearing his name still shows reruns all over the world every day, nearly 20 years since it aired its last episode! Jerry is undoubtedly very talented, except he wouldn't call it "talent." Jerry would call it skill—a skill that he honed and practiced over and over again.

One day, Brad Isaac, a journalist, asked Jerry Seinfeld what his secret was to becoming such a great comic. (The article of this exchange is published on Lifehacker.com under "Jerry Seinfeld's Productivity Secret.")

According to Brad, Jerry Seinfeld said that the only way to be a better comic is to write better jokes. And the only way to write better jokes is to write every day, and the only way to write every day is to have some method for keeping you consistent.

It's the "writing every day" part that gets most people hung up on anything they do when they are a *fish out of water*. But Jerry Seinfeld shared the secret to getting himself to write every day. Jerry wouldn't just track how many good jokes he wrote. Instead, it would actually measure how many days in a row he wrote. It didn't matter how good or bad the content was. The important thing was to do what was 100% in his control, and that was simply to write!

This is how it worked for Jerry. He would get a big wall calendar that shows the whole year. Then he'd have a big red marker. For each day that he wrote, he got to put a big red "X" on that day. After a few days or weeks, it would have a long chain of Xs. He said your mind likes seeing that chain. Then his whole job became this: *"don't break the chain."*

What I love about this method from Jerry Seinfeld, and in fact, all sharks, is how simple they keep things. This way of tracking and

measuring is also 100% in your control. As a
little side note, I personally adopted this
Seinfeld strategy of tracking and measuring
two years ago with my fitness. I used to
struggle with staying in shape, and working
out. Using this method of putting a big red X
on a calendar I went from working out
sporadically at best, to working out every day
for two years—and counting. It works.

What's actually happening here? How do
the most successful people keep winning
again and again? Guppies just go with the
flow in their little fishbowl they call life.
Sharks, on the other hand, measure and track
the key items in their life. Measuring and
tracking is a way sharks hold themselves
accountable, and it also shows where they can
improve.

One day I was talking with a millionaire
business mentor and I explained how I wasn't
getting the results I wanted. I needed some
advice. He immediately asked me, "How are
you measuring it?"

"Huh?" I thought. Admittedly, I wasn't
really systematically tracking anything.

"Calvin," he said, "you can't know if
you're winning unless you keep score. And

you can't improve it if you're not measuring it." That was a light-bulb moment! We went on to have a conversation about the types of things to measure. By "conversation" I mostly mean he talked, and I listened. He cautioned me to make sure I measure the *right* things.

"How can I measure the wrong things?" I asked.

"Measuring the wrong things is what most people do, and that's what keeps them stuck," he said.

"What do you mean?"

"Here's the rule of thumb: **you get more of what you measure.** So it's important you measure what you want *more* of, not *less* of. For example, let's say someone wants to get out of debt. Really, they don't want to 'get out of debt,' they want to be financially independent. But they're taught to count the debt, so they actually end up hanging onto the debt longer than they should, or worse, getting deeper into debt. Or if someone is trying to get into better shape what do they do? They stand on the scale and measure how many pounds they are. Instead, they should measure something like how many pounds *lost*—something they want more of."

In earlier chapters, you learned how important it is to focus on the right things—the things within your control. The same is true when it comes to what you track and measure. Most people tend to only measure what's called a "lag measure." In *The 4 Disciplines of Execution*, Sean Covey explains that a lag measure is something that's outside of your control. It's the final result. It's how many pounds you lost. It's the final score to a game. It's how much money you made in commission. The problem with this kind of scoring is once you get the number the game is already over. The information isn't very useful. You either won or lost. Okay, now what? What do you adjust?

Instead of simply counting the final score, sharks measure what Sean Covey calls a "lead measure." A lead measure is the actual thing that caused the result. It's something directly within your control. This is what sharks measure and track. Jerry Seinfeld didn't just track the number of good jokes he had. He understood that good jokes came through simply writing. So he measured how many days in a row he could write. This is how they keep score. This isn't saying that measuring the result, the lag measure, is a bad thing. It can be a clue to see that you're on the right track. But you just can't directly affect it immediately. So you must measure the actions and items within your control. Instead of just measuring how much weight you lost this week, you measure how many times you worked out. Working out is a lead measure because it's something you directly control, and it affects the lag measure.

You know you have a good lead measure when it directly affects the result. Working out more will positively affect how much weight you lose. Making more cold-calls can increase the number of sales you make. If you attend more networking events you're likely to increase your number of contacts. As a comedian, the number of days you write in a row can increase the number of great jokes you have. All of these are great lead measures. This was the secret of the shark and comedian Jerry Seinfeld.

So whatever it is you want to achieve, behave like a shark. Measure what you want more of, and make certain you don't only measure your results, measure the lead measure—the thing 100% in your control.

BOTTOM LINE: You can't know if you're winning if you don't keep score. Sharks measure and track the key items in their life. You get more of what you measure. Measure and track the things 100% in your control that will directly affect the result.

For bonus material on this chapter, go to
TheFishOutOfWaterBook.com/Measure

CHAPTER 11

FINAL THOUGHTS

Congratulations for coming this far! I know one thing: you have big goals and dreams in life. It's those of us who dare to dream big that make the difference. It's the sharks that cause change and make the world a better place. On this new journey, you are challenging the status quo. This journey isn't easy. While on the path there will be plenty of naysayers, cynics and critics along the way. Pay them no minds. If anything, know that critics mean you are on the right track.

Theodore Roosevelt so perfectly described the critic and what you will face as a shark. **"It is not the critic who counts; not the man who points out how the strong man stumbles, or where the doer of deeds could have done them better. The credit belongs to the man who is actually in the** arena, whose face is marred by dust and sweat and blood; who strives valiantly; who errs, who comes short again and again, because there is no effort without error and shortcoming; but who does actually strive to do the deeds; who knows great enthusiasms, the great devotions; who spends himself in a worthy cause; who at the best knows in the end the triumph of high achievement, and who at the worst, if he fails, at least fails while daring greatly, so that his place shall never be with those cold and timid souls who neither know victory nor defeat."

For being someone who is on the path, for striving valiantly, for being is in the arena, I commend you. We're coming to the end of our journey together. I designed *Fish Out of Water* to be a quick read that could be consumed on a one-way plane trip. I hope these principles create light bulbs moments that you'll carry with you. Remember, when you're a *fish out of water*, you already made a decision to go after something bigger. It feels awkward and scary, and sometimes you feel like you can barely breathe. But when you feel that way, use these principles and I promise you will get through. You'll literally transform into the new you.

The three principles work hand in hand. When you use them together, they become the catalyst for your personal growth and transformation. They are the keys to achieving the level of success you've always wanted.

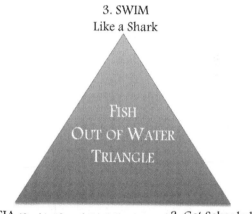

3. SWIM
Like a Shark

FISH
OUT OF WATER
TRIANGLE

1. CIA (Consistent Imperfect Action)   2. Get Schooled

Take consistent imperfect action.

Everything begins with action. Progress requires forward movement. Movement comes through action. You also learn better through action rather than reading about it! You can't learn deeply unless you are in the game. Learning comes through context, and context comes from playing. Don't let perfection hold you back from taking the action you know you need to take. Done is better than perfect. You can't adjust or get better if you aren't in the game. So whatever you do, commit to begin by taking action.

Get schooled.

You are the average of the five people you spend the most time with. If you hang out with five unhealthy people, chances are you'll be the sixth. But if you hang out with five athletes, chances are you'll be the sixth. Level up your influence. Don't spend time with guppies who are sitting in their fishbowl of mediocrity. Get around other *fish out of water,* and people living life at a higher level. Find a mentor, or hire a coach. Whatever you do, don't go it alone.

And finally, SWIM like a shark.

S – Success: put your focus of success on things inside your control. Focus on the actions, not the results. Know that success isn't something that happens later; success is in the moment. Focus on what's in your control and take action on those things. That will give you confidence, and increase your chances of accomplishing things that are currently outside of your control.

W – Words: What you say matters. Your words have power. Upgrade your language. Don't use fluffy words. Use empowering words of certainty.

I – Improve: Continue to sharpen your saw. Improve yourself. Make personal development a priority. Read books, attend workshops or seminars. Continually get better.

M – Measure: You get more of what you measure. Measure the key factors that will push you toward the goal. Measure things 100% inside your control.

"Greatness is not this wonderful, esoteric, illusive, godlike feature that only the special among us will ever taste. It's something that truly exists in all of us." – Will Smith.

There's a final secret I want to share with you before we end: you are already a shark. All of the successful people you read about in this book, or other sharks you see on TV, or social media, are no different than you. They were not born in special circumstances. They're not necessarily more talented. Sharks are regular people just like you. You already are a shark. Going through the process is just the way to let the shark come out.

In an interview, Will Smith was asked what's makes him different from the rest— how he achieved the level of success he has now. "The only thing I see that is distinctly different about me," Will Smith answered, "is I am not afraid to die on a treadmill. You might have more talent than me, you might be smarter than me, you might be sexier than me, you might be all those things better than me in nine categories. But, if we get on the treadmill together there are two options: either you're getting off first, or I'm going to die. It's really that simple." In other words, when Will Smith makes a decision he's going stick to it. He's going to see it through. He's going to continue to take action.

That is what makes a shark a shark. If there's one thing you take from this book it's this—successful people are no different than you. You are just as powerful as they are. I mean that! Every shark went through the *fish out of water* process. They did stuff that didn't feel natural to them. They had fears.

They weren't perfect. They were *human*. This was a huge breakthrough for me! I used to put successful people up high on a pedestal and think that there was something special about them that wasn't special about me. But I'm here to tell you, that's not the case.

Steve Jobs put it this way. "When you grow up you tend to get told that the world is the way that it is. Your life is just to try to live within the world without bashing into the walls too much. But that's a very limited life. Life can be so much broader when you discover one simple fact: everything around you that you call life *was made up by people that were no smarter than you*. You can change it. You can influence it. You can build your own things for other people to use. Once you learn that, you'll never be the same again."

It's my hope you continue to discover the power you already have.

I love success stories! Go to TheFishOutOfWaterBook.com to submit yours. I look forward to hearing from you.

May you never be the same again. Listen to your heart, and go make *your* ding in the universe.

ABOUT THE AUTHOR

CALVIN WAYMAN is a social media entrepreneur. He founded *CobbesMedia*, a social media management agency for influencers, thought-leaders and entrepreneurs. Calvin's passion is helping entrepreneurs make an impact on the world through modern tools and technology. Calvin currently lives in Northern Arizona with his wife Bekah, and his son Archie.

Made in the USA
Lexington, KY
02 July 2017